Wolfgang Amadeus
MOZART

(1756 – 1791)

Concerto for Violin and Orchestra, KV 216
G Major / Sol majeur / G-Dur

Edited by
Herbert Scherz

DOWANI International

Preface

This edition presents a piece that belongs in the standard repertoire of every violinist: the Concerto for violin and orchestra KV 216 in G Major by Wolfgang Amadeus Mozart. It allows you to work through the piece systematically and at different tempi with accompaniment.

The CD begins with the concert version of each movement. After tuning your instrument (Track 1), the musical work can begin. First, you will hear the piano accompaniment at slow and medium tempo for practice purposes. At slow tempo you can also hear the violin played softly in the background as a guide. Having mastered these levels, you can now play the piece with orchestra at the original tempo. Only in the concert version are the cadenzas played complete. The practice tempos give you time to play a very short cadenza in each movement concerned; the entrance following the cadenza can be found with the aid of a metronome click. All of the versions were recorded live. The names of the musicians are listed on the last page of this volume; further information can be found in the Internet at www.dowani.com.

The fingering and bowing marks in our volume were provided by Herbert Scherz, a renowned violin teacher who for many years was professor of violin and violin methodology at the conservatories in Lucerne and Zurich. Today, after his retirement, he continues to teach very successfully on a private basis. His pupils have won more than 150 prizes at violin and chamber music competitions; many of them now have successful international careers. In 1985 he founded the "Lucerne Ministrings", an ensemble of children and teenagers up to the age of 16 that has given many concerts in Switzerland and abroad.

We wish you lots of fun playing from our *DOWANI 3 Tempi Play Along* editions and hope that your musicality and diligence will enable you to play the concert version as soon as possible.

It is our goal to give you the essential conditions for effective practicing through motivation, enjoyment and fun.

Your DOWANI Team

Avant-propos

Cette édition vous présente un morceau qui fait partie du répertoire standard de tous les violonistes : le concerto pour violon et orchestre KV 216 en Sol majeur de Wolfgang Amadeus Mozart. Cette édition vous offre la possibilité de travailler l'œuvre d'une manière systématique dans différents tempos avec un accompagnement professionnel.

Le CD vous permettra d'entendre d'abord la version de concert de chaque mouvement. Après avoir accordé votre instrument (plage N° 1), vous pourrez commencer le travail musical. Pour travailler le morceau au tempo lent et au tempo moyen, vous entendrez l'accompagnement de piano. Au tempo lent, le violon restera cependant toujours audible très doucement à l'arrière-plan. Vous pourrez ensuite jouer le tempo original avec accompagnement d'orchestre. Les cadences entières ont été enregistrées seulement dans la version de concert. Aux tempos de travail, vous aurez le temps de jouer une très brève cadence ; le métronome vous aidera à trouver l'attaque après la cadence. Toutes les versions ont été enregistrées en direct. Vous trouverez les noms des artistes qui ont participé aux enregistrements sur la dernière page de cette édition ; pour obtenir plus de renseignements, veuillez consulter notre site Internet : www.dowani.com.

Les doigtés et indications des coups d'archet proviennent de Herbert Scherz, violoniste et pédagogue de grande renommée. Il fut pendant de nombreuses années professeur de violon et de la méthodique de violon aux Conservatoires Supérieurs de Musique à Lucerne et Zurich et donne depuis sa retraite toujours des cours privés avec grand succès. Ses élèves ont reçus plus de 150 prix aux concours de violon et de musique de chambre et beaucoup d'entre eux ont

du succès au niveau international. En 1985, il fonda les "Ministrings Luzern", un ensemble d'enfants et de jeunes jusqu'à 16 ans qui donne de nombreux concerts en Suisse et à l'etranger.

Nous vous souhaitons beaucoup de plaisir à faire de la musique avec la collection *DOWANI 3 Tempi Play Along* et nous espérons que votre musicalité et votre application vous amèneront aussi rapidement que possible à la version de concert.

Notre but est de vous offrir les bases nécessaires pour un travail efficace par la motivation et le plaisir.

Les Éditions DOWANI

Vorwort

Mit dieser Ausgabe präsentieren wir Ihnen ein Stück, das zum Standardrepertoire eines jeden Geigers zählt: das Konzert für Violine und Orchester KV 216 in G-Dur von Wolfgang Amadeus Mozart. Diese Ausgabe ermöglicht es Ihnen, das Werk systematisch und in verschiedenen Tempi mit Begleitung zu erarbeiten.

Auf der CD hören Sie zuerst die Konzertversion eines jeden Satzes. Nach dem Stimmen Ihres Instrumentes (Track 1) kann die musikalische Arbeit beginnen. Zum Üben folgt nun im langsamen und mittleren Tempo die Klavierbegleitung, wobei im langsamen Tempo die Violine als Orientierung leise im Hintergrund zu hören ist. Anschließend können Sie sich im Originaltempo vom Orchester begleiten lassen. Die Kadenzen werden nur in der Konzertversion komplett gespielt. Bei den Übe-Tempi haben Sie jeweils Zeit für eine sehr kurze Kadenz; den Einsatz nach der Kadenz finden Sie mit Hilfe von Metronomklicks. Alle eingespielten Versionen wurden live aufgenommen. Die Namen der Künstler finden Sie auf der letzten Seite dieser Ausgabe; ausführlichere

Informationen können Sie im Internet unter www.dowani.com nachlesen.

Die Fingersätze und Bogenstriche in dieser Ausgabe stammen von dem renommierten Violinpädagogen Herbert Scherz. Er war viele Jahre als Professor für Violine und Violinmethodik an den Musikhochschulen in Luzern und Zürich tätig und unterrichtet seit seiner Pensionierung auch heute noch sehr erfolgreich als Privatlehrer. Seine Schüler haben über 150 Preise bei Violin- und Kammermusikwettbewerben erhalten und viele von ihnen sind inzwischen auf internationaler Ebene sehr erfolgreich. 1985 gründete er die „Ministrings Luzern", ein Ensemble mit Kindern und Jugendlichen bis 16 Jahren, das zahlreiche Konzerte im In- und Ausland gibt.

Wir wünschen Ihnen viel Spaß beim Musizieren aus *DOWANI 3 Tempi Play Along*-Ausgaben und hoffen, dass Ihre Musikalität und Ihr Fleiß Sie möglichst bald bis zur Konzertversion führen werden.

Unser Ziel ist es, Ihnen durch Motivation, Freude und Spaß die notwendigen Voraussetzungen für effektives Üben zu schaffen.

Ihr DOWANI Team

Concerto

for Violin and Orchestra, KV 216
G Major / Sol majeur / G-Dur

W. A. Mozart (1756 – 1791)
Piano Reduction: G. Stöver

DOW 04507

Wolfgang Amadeus MOZART

(1756 – 1791)

Concerto for Violin and Orchestra, KV 216
G Major / Sol majeur / G-Dur

Violin / Violon / Violine

DOWANI International

Rondo

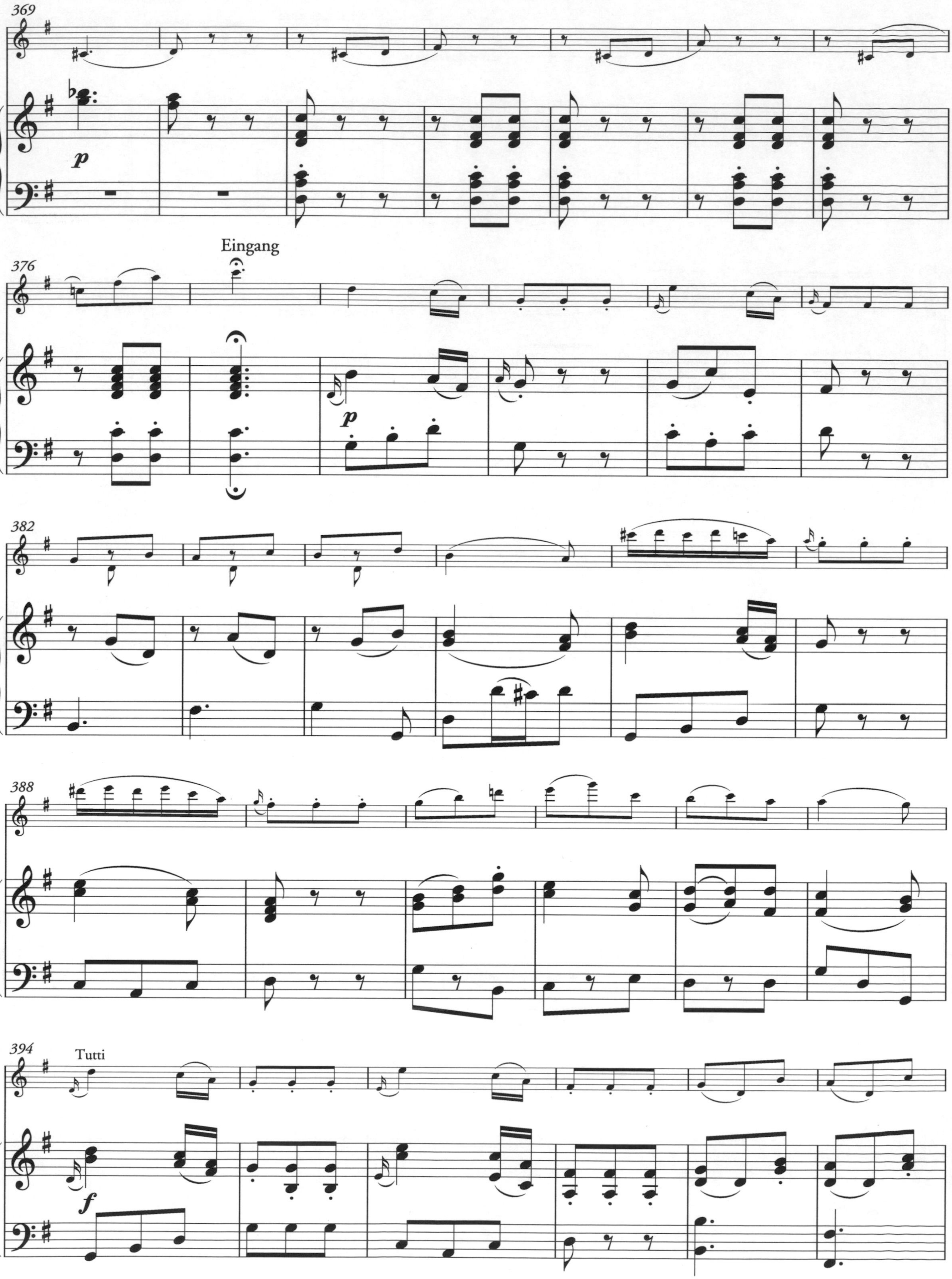
Eingang
Tutti

ENGLISH

DOWANI CD:
- Track No. 1

  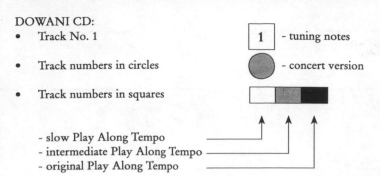

  1 - tuning notes
- Track numbers in circles

  ⬤ - concert version
- Track numbers in squares

  ▭▨▮

  - slow Play Along Tempo
  - intermediate Play Along Tempo
  - original Play Along Tempo

- Additional tracks for longer movements or pieces
- **Double CD:** CD1 = A, CD2 = B
- **Concert version:** violin and orchestra
- **Slow tempo:** piano accompaniment with violin in the background
- **Intermediate tempo:** piano accompaniment only
- **Original tempo:** orchestra only

Please note that the recorded version of the piano accompaniment may differ slightly from the sheet music. This is due to the spontaneous character of live music making and the artistic freedom of the musicians. The original sheet music for the solo part is, of course, not affected.

Cadenzas: The full cadenzas are only played in the concert version.

FRANÇAIS

DOWANI CD:
- Plage N° 1

  1 - diapason
- N° de plage dans un cercle

  ⬤ - version de concert
- N° de plage dans un rectangle

  ▭▨▮

  - tempo lent play along
  - tempo moyen play along
  - tempo original play along

- Plages supplémentaires pour mouvements ou morceaux longs
- **Double CD:** CD1 = A, CD2 = B
- **Version de concert :** violon avec accompagnement d'orchestre
- **Tempo lent :** accompagnement de piano avec violon en fond sonore
- **Tempo moyen :** seulement l'accompagnement de piano
- **Tempo original :** seulement l'accompagnement de l'orchestre

L'enregistrement de l'accompagnement de piano peut présenter quelques différences mineures par rapport au texte de la partition. Ceci est du à la liberté artistique des musiciens et résulte d'un jeu spontané et vivant, mais n'affecte, bien entendu, d'aucune manière la partie soliste.

Cadences: Les cadences entières ont été enregistrées seulement dans la version de concert.

DEUTSCH

DOWANI CD:
- Track Nr. 1

  1 - Stimmtöne
- Trackangabe im Kreis

  ⬤ - Konzertversion
- Trackangabe im Rechteck

  ▭▨▮

  - langsames Play Along Tempo
  - mittleres Play Along Tempo
  - originales Play Along Tempo

- Zusätzliche Tracks bei längeren Sätzen oder Stücken
- **Doppel-CD:** CD1 = A, CD2 = B
- **Konzertversion:** Violine und Orchester
- **Langsames Tempo:** Klavierbegleitung mit Violine im Hintergrund
- **Mittleres Tempo:** nur Klavierbegleitung
- **Originaltempo:** nur Orchester

Die Klavierbegleitung auf der CD-Aufnahme kann gegenüber dem Notentext kleine Abweichungen aufweisen. Dies geht in der Regel auf die künstlerische Freiheit der Musiker und auf spontanes, lebendiges Musizieren zurück. Die Solostimme bleibt davon selbstverständlich unangetastet.

Kadenzen: Die Kadenzen sind nur in der Konzertversion komplett eingespiel

DOWANI - 3 Tempi Play Along is published by:
DOWANI International
A division of De Haske (International) AG
Postfach 60, CH-6332 Hagendorn
Switzerland
Phone: +41-(0)41-785 82 50 / Fax: +41-(0)41-785 82 58
Email: info@dowani.com
www.dowani.com

Recording & Digital Mastering: Pavel Lavrenenkov, Russia
Music Notation: Notensatz Thomas Metzinger, Germany
Design: Atelier Schuster, Austria

Concert Version
Alexander Trostyansky, Violin
Russian Philharmonic Orchestra Moscow
Boris Perrenoud, Conductor

3 Tempi Accompaniment
Slow:
Tatyana Gevorkova, Piano

Intermediate:
Tatyana Gevorkova, Piano

Original:
Russian Philharmonic Orchestra Moscow
Boris Perrenoud, Conductor